Editor-in-Chief and Founder:
 Lyndon H. LaRouche, Jr.
Editorial Board: *Lyndon H. LaRouche, Jr. , Helga
 Zepp-LaRouche, Robert Ingraham, Tony
 Papert, Gerald Rose, Dennis Small, Jeffrey
 Steinberg, William Wertz*
Co-Editors: *Robert Ingraham, Tony Papert*
Managing Editor: *Nancy Spannaus*
Technology: *Marsha Freeman*
Books: *Katherine Notley*
Ebooks: *Richard Burden*
Graphics: *Alan Yue*
Photos: *Stuart Lewis*
Circulation Manager: *Stanley Ezrol*

INTELLIGENCE DIRECTORS
Counterintelligence: *Jeffrey Steinberg, Michele
 Steinberg*
Economics: *John Hoefle, Marcia Merry Baker,
 Paul Gallagher*
History: *Anton Chaitkin*
Ibero-America: *Dennis Small*
Russia and Eastern Europe: *Rachel Douglas*
United States: *Debra Freeman*

INTERNATIONAL BUREAUS
Bogotá: *Miriam Redondo*
Berlin: *Rainer Apel*
Copenhagen: *Tom Gillesberg*
Houston: *Harley Schlanger*
Lima: *Sara Madueño*
Melbourne: *Robert Barwick*
Mexico City: *Gerardo Castilleja Chávez*
New Delhi: *Ramtanu Maitra*
Paris: *Christine Bierre*
Stockholm: *Ulf Sandmark*
United Nations, N.Y.C.: *Leni Rubinstein*
Washington, D.C.: *William Jones*
Wiesbaden: *Göran Haglund*

ON THE WEB
e-mail: eirns@larouchepub.com
www.larouchepub.com
www.executiveintelligencereview.com
www.larouchepub.com/eiw
Webmaster: *John Sigerson*
Assistant Webmaster: *George Hollis*
Editor, Arabic-language edition: *Hussein Askary*

EIR (ISSN 0273-6314) *is published weekly
(50 issues), by EIR News Service, Inc.,
P.O. Box 17390, Washington, D.C. 20041-0390.
(703) 777-9451*

European Headquarters: E.I.R. GmbH, Postfach
Bahnstrasse 9a, D-65205, Wiesbaden, Germany
Tel: 49-611-73650
Homepage: http://www.eirna.com
e-mail: eirna@eirna.com
Director: Georg Neudecker

Montreal, Canada: 514-461-1557

Denmark: EIR - Danmark, Sankt Knuds Vej 11,
basement left, DK-1903 Frederiksberg, Denmark.
Tel.: +45 35 43 60 40, Fax: +45 35 43 87 57. e-mail:
eirdk@hotmail.com.

Mexico City: EIR, Sor Juana Inés de la Cruz 242-2
Col. Agricultura C.P. 11360
Delegación M. Hidalgo, México D.F.
Tel. (5525) 5318-2301
eirmexico@gmail.com

Canada Post Publication Sales Agreement
#40683579

Postmaster: Send all address changes to *EIR*, P.O.
Box 17390, Washington, D.C. 20041-0390.

Signed articles in *EIR* represent the views of the
authors, and not necessarily those of the Editorial
Board.

World War III
Is at Our Doorstep

Editorial

Expose the Saudi-British Role In 9/11! Dump Obama Now!

Host Matthew Ogden began the LaRouche PAC International Webcast of April 29 by quoting from an April 28 National Public Radio interview with former Senator Bob Graham, who was the co-chairman of the Joint Congressional Inquiry into 9/11. Ogden then summarized what Lyndon LaRouche had said after hearing that interview.

Senator Graham:

The reason why the 28 pages are so important is that they were the conclusion of the congressional inquiry into 9/11 as to how that plot was financed. Who paid for it? And while I can't discuss the details of that chapter, they point a strong finger at Saudi Arabia.

What we do know publicly was that there were agents of the Saudi government which assisted at least two of the hijackers who ended up living in San Diego—provided them with financial support, with anonymity, with a place to live and with flight lessons, and protected them for, in one case, over a year. The FBI has turned over to a federal court, through a Freedom of Information Act case, 80,000 pages involving an investigation that took place in Sarasota, Florida, of the relationship between Mohammed Atta, the leader of the 19 hijackers, and two of his henchmen, and a prominent Saudi family, which had lived in Sarasota for six years. Two weeks before 9/11 they left under what were described as urgent conditions to return to Saudi Arabia, creating the inference that they were tipped off and decided they would be better off someplace else than in Sarasota when 9/11 occurred.

NPR asked Graham: "Do you believe that consecutive administrations have been protecting the Saudi royal family against the interests of United States citizens?"

Yes. And I think it's been more than a cover-up. I think it's been what I call aggressive deception. There are instances in which the FBI has publicly released statements which I know from personal experience were untrue. They stated that in this Sarasota situation, they had completed the investigation, that the investigation determined that there were no connections between the hijackers and the prominent Saudi family, and that they had turned over all of this information to both the congressional inquiry and the 9/11 Commission. I know for a fact that none of those three statements is true.

NPR: "Let me get this right, sir. You are alleging that the FBI deliberately lied about this issue and that there has been a cover-up."

Sen. Graham interrupted to say: "It's more than a cover-up. The FBI misstated what is in their own records relative to the situation in Sarasota."

He was asked: "What do you think needs to happen?"

He replied: "I think we need to have a general reopening of the investigation into 9/11. Both the Congressional [Inquiry] and the 9/11 Commission operated under tight time restraints, which precluded the full inquiry that needs to be held when the 9/11 issue is reopened."

Mr. LaRouche said, after listening to this interview, that this is cut and dried. it cannot be argued with. Everything that Sen. Graham said was absolutely right. He said,

Justice must finally be served to the citizens of the United States. It can no longer be postponed. Nobody can say, "Let's just put this off, let's put this off, let's put this off for another week." *It must happen now*. The true story has been covered up for far too long. Sen. Graham's statements on this are cut and dried. His identification of the "aggressive deception" by the FBI goes right to the point, and cannot be argued with. Remember, the FBI is under the jurisdiction of the Justice Department, which is a member of the Executive Branch, which places this entire operation right on Obama's doorstep. The Executive Branch can't act without the President's direct orders.

Any attempt to perpetuate this is a violation of the Constitutional rights of the citizens of the United States, in the interests of what is proved to be a hostile, foreign, power, right up to the point of what could be called approaching treason. The danger is that of World War III, which would threaten the destruction of not only the United States, but the entire world. Not a day goes by that there is not a provocation occurring somewhere in the world by Obama against both Russia and China, any one of which could light the fuse for World War III. We cannot wait, we cannot put things off. We can't say, "Oh, just a few more weeks, just a few more months." World War III is at our doorstep, and World War III would mean the destruction of the human race.

The ceasefire in Syria is nearing the point of disintegration. The role of Saudi Arabia and Turkey in this is apparent and a very obvious point, and the strategic leverage that is needed through the declassification of the 28 pages, would stop this war. This shows you just one example—a very immediate example—but this is just one example of the strategic necessity of releasing the 28 pages and exposing the Saudis and their partners in the British monarchy for what they are and what they did in the case of the crime of 9/11.

EIR Contents

www.larouchepub.com Volume 43, Number 19, May 6, 2016

Cover This Week

U.S. Army soldier fires an M320 grenade launcher in an Estonia Army Training Area, Nov. 2, 2015, as part of the U.S. Army Europe-led Operation Atlantic Resolve land force assurance training.

Tenth Press Camp Headquarters/Sgt. First Class Ernest White

I. Obama Goes to War

NATO'S NEW OPERATION BARBAROSSA

What Business Does the German Military Have in Lithuania?

by Helga Zepp-LaRouche, chairman of the German political party BüSo

April 30—If you look at the range of NATO's actions against Russia, as well as those of the U.S. armed forces against China, a picture of deliberate encirclement and provocation emerges, whose only result will be a great catastrophe. For example: The German government now proposes to station soldiers in Lithuania as part of NATO's thousand-man battalion—71 years after Hitler's crushing defeat in his demented expedition against the Soviet Union. That is simply scandalous.

After President Obama signaled, prior to his recent visit to Hannover, that he expected greater military engagement and funding from Germany, German Chancellor Angela Merkel found nothing better to do than to pledge this contribution of troops at the mini-summit in Hannover of the heads of government of Great Britain, Germany, France, and Italy with Obama. This "permanent rotating mission" is expected to be finalized at the coming NATO summit in Warsaw in early July, along with an array of other offensive measures against Russia.

At the Moscow Security Conference of April 27-28, Russian Ambassador to NATO Alexander Grushko warned against the consequences of NATO's policy of confrontation on Russia's western

flank—including measures such as the "permanent troop rotation" (of which the German troop deployment is to be only a part), the permanent relocation of heavy weapons systems to eastern European countries, endless maneuvers, continuous air surveillance, and the reinforcement of naval forces in the Baltic and Black Seas.

In the latest incident in the Baltic—when Russian fighter aircraft flew over U.S. warships operating about 75 miles off the coast of Kaliningrad, the Russian enclave between Poland and Lithuania—the U.S. side invoked what it calls "anti-access/area denial" (A2AD)

Bundesregierung/GüngörGrossansicht

Obama and Merkel hold a press conference on April 26 at Obama's mini-summit in Hannover. She said "yes."

The German government plans to send troops to Lithuania as part of a NATO battalion of a thousand men. Here, Soviet troops mop up remnants of resistance on Jan. 31, 1943, after defeating the German Army at Stalingrad.

under the pretext that Russia was denying free access to NATO's military support for the Baltic states. In fact, NATO was questioning Russia's right to self-defense in the immediate vicinity of its borders.

Also in process is the formation of military brigades comprising troops from Bulgaria, Romania, and Ukraine, or Lithuania, Poland, and Ukraine. The expansion of the U.S. Ballistic Missile System into Eastern Europe is also going forward, although after the "P5+1" agreement with Iran, any pretext that this system is for defense against Iranian missiles has been dropped. It is perfectly clear that the system is oriented toward neutralizing Russia's nuclear second-strike capability.

See No Evil

Virtually no one in Germany asks why the Obama Administration intends to spend a trillion dollars (a trillion!) in the coming years on the modernization of the entire U.S. nuclear weapons arsenal—including the B61-12 tactical nuclear weapons to be stationed in Germany—an action which would make them (along with the stealth bombers) "operational," as was recently pointed out in a U.S. Senate hearing by Sen. Dianne Feinstein. That no one in Germany questions this, can only be explained as collective paralysis and amnesia. All of this is happening in an environment that U.S.

military analysts such as Ted Postol and Hans Kristensen have identified as more dangerous than at the high point of the Cold War, namely the Cuban Missile Crisis. That is why figures such as Mikhail Gorbachev and the recently deceased Helmut Schmidt warned not long ago of the danger of a Third World War.

This time the overeager obedience of Mrs. Merkel and the fealty of the careerist military have gone too far. Germany is increasingly involved in NATO's encirclement strategy against Russia, moving NATO ever closer to Russia's borders, not Russia moving westward as claimed. (Russian Foreign Minister Sergey Lavrov called that claim a "dirty attempt to turn reality on its head.") Germany's involvement puts its very existence at risk: In a nuclear war, nothing will remain of Germany, and no one would be left alive. No one can convince us that Mrs. Merkel, Defense Minister Ursula von der Leyen, and the military leadership are not perfectly aware of that.

Along with the NATO operations against Russia are the U.S. armed forces' escalating provocations against China. The United States insists on "freedom of the seas" in the South China Sea—although China has not once hindered passage—a demand the United States uses to justify flights over contested islands and reefs in violation of Chinese territory. Then there is the attempt to use the crisis over North Korea to station the THAAD missile defense system in South Korea, a system that threatens Russia and China, and the deployment of an additional 250 U.S. Special Forces personnel to Syria without Syrian government invitation, without a UN Security Council mandate, and without the authorization of the U.S. Congress as required by the American Constitution.

A Policy of Brinksmanship

These are all elements of a policy of brinksmanship. Are they designed to lure Russia and China into a trap and provoke reactions which can be used as a pretext for large-scale punitive actions? Is it a deployment for a first strike, in accordance with U.S. war doctrines such as Prompt Global Strike and Air-Sea Battle? Is it seriously believed that the costs of a new arms race, combined with color revolutions, will result in regime change in Moscow and Beijing, because the people will rise up against Vladimir Putin and Xi Jinping? All of these scenarios are insane. In every case they risk the obliteration of mankind in a global thermonuclear war.

It is not Russia and China that are the problem, but the neo-liberal financial policy which underlies the supposed necessity for the imperial expansion of the trans-Atlantic sector. The commitment to this policy is the underlying reason that no one addresses the *causes* of refugee flight in the refugee crisis; those causes are the result of the wars in Southwest Asia based on lies, and a policy that has denied development to Africa through the imposition of the notorious IMF conditionalities. It is this policy which has intolerably widened the gap between rich and poor in many parts of the world, and which seems ready to sacrifice everything to the Moloch of high-risk speculation for the advantage of the few, at the expense of the many. And even this policy is hopelessly bankrupt, as the lunatic debate about "helicopter money" shows.

Just the idea—71 years after the total defeat of the Nazis, who inflicted untold suffering on the Russian people and many others, including our own—that we Germans could participate in a new Operation Barbarossa against Russia, must be rejected in the strongest terms and in practice. If the escalations now planned—including the granting of NATO special status to Ukraine and Georgia as "associate partners," long identified by Russia as a red line, possible NATO membership for Finland and Sweden, and the deployment of German forces to Lithuania—are adopted at the upcoming NATO summit, then in all probability we will find ourselves on the direct road to Hell.

The Alternative

We must therefore use the remaining two months before the summit to get the alternative underway. That means win-win cooperation with Russia and China, without which none of the life-or-death problems facing us—the war danger, the impending financial crash, the refugee crisis, and terrorism—can be solved. And we can show no greater friendship to the true United States than by insisting on this cooperation.

There is a way out. We must join with Russia, China, and India in building the New Silk Road to ensure the economic development of Southwest Asia and Africa, and the reconstruction of our own productive economy. We must make it clear to the United States that we are not willing to commit suicide to maintain an empire. For the America of George Washington, Alexander Hamilton, Abraham Lincoln, Franklin D. Roosevelt, and John F. Kennedy, however, a place of honor is reserved in the community of nations.

This article was written for the May 4 issue of Neue Solidarität *and has been translated from the German.*

Prelude to War in the Pacific

by William Jones

April 30—President Obama's provocative policy in the Pacific is leading to a conflict between nuclear powers, and can have no other result if the policy is not quickly reversed. These provocations have gone so far as sailing destroyers straight into waters legitimately claimed as territorial waters by the People's Republic of China, in alleged "freedom of navigation" patrols, and attempts to line up local "allies" to join in. While the naval deployments are accompanied by all sorts of high-falutin' moralizing rhetoric from the U.S. government, in reality they have less justification than the European gunboats on the Yangtze in the 19th Century.

In response to Chinese attempts to assert their legitimate claims to the Nansha (Spratly) and the Xisha (Paracel) Islands, the United States has organized joint sorties with its "ally," the Philippines, to patrol the seas right up to the 12-mile limit off the shore of the Chinese mainland. Obama refers to a supposed threat to "freedom of navigation," but China has never threatened or contested that freedom in the South China Sea,— where the overwhelming majority of all navigation is to and from China itself.

Freedom of Navigation or Gunboat Diplomacy?

Freedom of navigation in non-territorial waters has long been a staple of maritime law, from Hugo Grotius' classic *Law of the Seas* to the more recent UN Law of the Sea Convention (UNCLOS). When the UNCLOS Treaty was promulgated in 1982, the United States did not sign it, ostensibly because of the limitations the treaty would place on its offshore drilling operations.

In reality, the United States had already, during the Carter Administration, pre-empted joining such a treaty by elaborating what it called its Freedom of Navigation Policy, which in effect guaranteed the right of U.S. naval vessels to sail freely anywhere in the world that was not considered sovereign territory (that is, within 12 miles of any country's land borders). This included freely sailing within any country's Exclusive Economic Zone (EEZ, defined by the UNCLOS as a region within 200 miles of a country's land border). While the UNCLOS also allows "innocent passage" within the EEZ for mili-

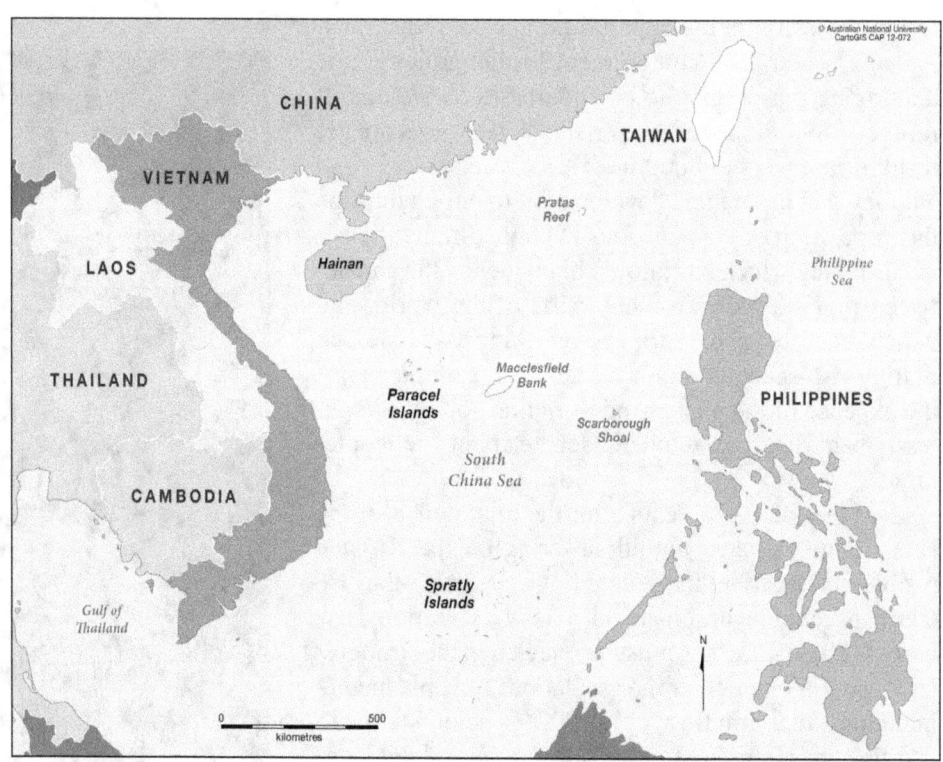

Obama's provocative policy challenging China's legitimate claims to the Spratly and Paracel Islands includes patrolling, jointly with its "ally" the Philippines, right up to the 12-mile limit off the shore of the Chinese mainland.

U.S. Airforce/Senior Master Sgt. Adrian Cadiz

The United States' unilateral Freedom of Navigation Policy allows the U.S. Navy to sail whenever and wherever it wants. These types of military maneuvers have been ratcheted up to the highest level ever by Obama. Above, U.S. Navy sailors, on April 15, are carrying out flight deck operations in the South China Sea on aircraft carrier USS John C. Stennis while Secretary of Defense Ash Carter and Philippine Secretary of National Defense Voltaire Gazmin are on board as observers.

tary vessels that are not conducting military or reconnaissance operations, the treaty does not prevent a country from requiring notification of such passage.

The U.S. policy effectively allows the U.S. Navy to sail wherever and whenever it wants, unimpeded by the strictures of any treaty. The Freedom of Navigation forays have often been used to warn nations against any restriction on the "innocent passage" of U.S. military vessels, essentially making them a modern form of "gunboat diplomacy," even though no shots have been fired—at least not yet. But those operations have never before been ratcheted up in the way they are now by the Obama Administration against China in the South China Sea.

China's Territorial Claims

The Western media, in their typical manner, have depicted China's claims to the Nansha (Spratly) and Xisha (Paracel) Islands as a Chinese "power grab," although for most of China's history, these claims have never been contested. In the 1970s—with the growth in the importance of the seabeds for offshore drilling and the expansion of the fishing industry with a diminishing fish population—other countries in the region have raised their own claims to the islands, and the Philippines, Vietnam, and Malaysia all began, with the help

of their militaries, to build facilities on some of the islands, which China solemnly protested at the time.

After World War II, the United States fully supported China in reclaiming these islands from Japan. But the Cold War and the peaceful rise of China to become a world power have changed all of that. And recent U.S. actions have effectively sent signals to China that the United States will not accept the Chinese claims and is prepared to go to war to prevent China from asserting them, despite Obama's hollow pretense that the United States is not taking sides with respect to those claims.

As early as the Han Dynasty (206 BC-220 AD), the islands are found in Chinese records, clearly documentating their recognition, and perhaps their discovery, by the Chinese. They were incorporated into the administrative region of Qiong Zhou during the Tang Dynasty (618-907 AD) and further consolidated into the Chinese Empire during the Yuan Dynasty (1271-1368).

Later, during the Ming and Qing Dynasties (1368-1912), the islands were incorporated into the administration of Wanzhou in Guangdong Province. During this time there were extensive activities by Chinese on the islands, including fishing and planting, and some Chinese even lived on the islands for years. Many Chinese relics and remains have been found there, including the remains of temples. During the Ming and Qing Dynasties, the Nansha (Spratly) and Xisha (Paracel) Islands were incorporated into the defense of the Chinese Empire, with regular patrols, coastal defense, and administration by China's naval forces.

When the Japanese moved into Southeast Asia in World War II, everything changed. The islands were occupied by Japan until the end of the war. After the war, it was clearly recognized by the Allied Powers that the islands were a part of Chinese territory and should be returned to China. Both the war-time Cairo Declaration and the subsequent Potsdam Declaration are explicit in their demand that Japan should give back these occupied islands to China.

In fact, the United States sent warships to the Kuomintang in 1946 to enable the recovery of the

Xinhua News Agency/Xing Guangli

This Chinese lighthouse on Zhubi Reef began operations in April. It is one of three China has built in the Nanshas (Spratly Islands). China has also set up emergency rescue facilities in the Spratly and Paracel Islands.

Nansha Islands! And books, periodicals, and maps published in the United States clearly indicated that the Nanshas are part of Chinese territory. While the San Francisco Treaty in 1951 also affirmed that Japan must give up the islands, it did not explicitly state that the territory belongs to China, an argument that is now being used by the Philippines to bolster its own claims. But China was not represented at all at that conference, and had no say in the formulation of the treaty. While the United States wished to invite Taiwan to represent China, Great Britain wanted the People's Republic of China, and the dispute resulted in no Chinese representative being invited.

But even after World War II, none of the present claimants challenged China's sovereignty over the islands. In 1955, the International Civil Aviation Organization, at its conference in Manila, asked Taiwan to improve meteorological observation on the Nansha Islands, with no objection from any of the participants.

Chinese possession of the islands would have a beneficial effect on navigation in the region. Already China has constructed two lighthouses on Huayang Reef in the Nanshas, and emergency rescue facilities have been established on the Nanshas and Xishas. So why is

Obama now so determinedly opposed to the Chinese claims?

Occupation of its coastal islands would definitely be beneficial to Chinese defense capabilities. Even if China did not decide to place military installations there, they would provide a somewhat more advanced perimeter from which to monitor any threats from the region. And given the increased U.S. naval deployments here, such a capability becomes of increasing importance for China.

Remember that the United States in 1872 sent General John Schofield to the then independent kingdom of Hawaii to investigate those islands for the purpose of eventually putting U.S. military facilities on an advanced perimeter in the Pacific. But the Hawaiian Islands are 2,390 miles from the coast of California, while the Nansha Islands are 500 miles from the Chinese coast and the Xisha only 180 miles. And while the United States had no claim to the Hawaiian islands (but would soon annex them in rather murky circumstances), China does have such a claim, a claim which was once universally recognized.

Sabotaging a Resolution of the Conflict

China is clearly aware of the conflicts that have arisen with its neighbors over its attempt to make good on its claims. It is also concerned to maintain amicable

In 1872, the United States sent General John Schofield to what was then the independent kingdom of Hawaii to investigate the Islands for purposes of establishing an advanced perimeter in the Pacific, 2,390 miles from the California coast, a far greater distance than that from China to the South China Sea Islands. The Islands were later annexed by the United States, though it had no claim to them.

relations with its neighbors, including those against whom China fought in the last great war. It is therefore engaged in coming to agreements with the various claimants through a process of bilateral negotiations.

The agreements between the countries of the region, encapsulated in the 2012 Declaration of Conduct signed by the members of ASEAN and the Government of China, therefore call on the parties "to resolve their territorial and jurisdictional disputes by peaceful means, without resorting to the threat or use of force, through friendly consultations and negotiations by sovereign states directly concerned, in accordance with universally recognized principles of international law, including the 1982 UN Convention on the Law of the Sea."

This declaration committed the parties to resolve their difference through bilateral negotiations. But the Philippines, in its dispute with China on one of the islands, has taken the issue to arbitration, with the blessing of the United States, hoping that the Permanent Court of Arbitration in the Hague will rule in its favor. China, which continues to adhere to the agreement signed in 2012, has clearly said that it is not prepared to accept any judgment stemming from such unilateral action on the part of the Philippines.

If the disputes involved only the countries in the region, they could be resolved amicably. Given the economic strength of China and its clear willingness to use that strength to create a win-win situation for its neighbors—as we have seen in China's "Belt and Road" Initiative—there is no reason that satisfactory arrangements beneficial to all could not be worked out.

One of the options that has often been put forward would involve joint ventures to exploit the mineral resources of the area. In fact, in 2004 the Philippines and China agreed to joint exploration for oil in the Nansha islands, and the exploration began, only to be sabotaged by a manipulated anti-China uproar in the Philippines. It was discussed again in 2013, only to be rejected by the Philippines under heavy pressure from Washington.

But the U.S. invasions of Chinese waters, and the attempts by the United States to create a mini-NATO to target China using the few allies it has in the region, have made such a solution all but impossible. And unless the war-mongering Barack Obama is soon removed from office for his crimes, and his policy reversed, we may be looking at another war in the Pacific—and the threat of a nuclear tsunami.

Virginia Senator Black: 'I Will Be Syria's Voice'

by Robert Ingraham

May 1—On April 26, 2016, Virginia State Senator Richard Black began a three-day visit to the nation of Syria. Prior to his trip, Black said in a letter that he was traveling to Syria "in an attempt to restore peace and prevent the slaughter of Christians and other minorities." During the trip, according to the Syrian Arab News Agency (SANA), Black also pledged that as soon as he returns to the United States, he will work towards organizing discussions in the Congress in order to change the prevailing view about what is happening in Syria, that he will work to lift the sanctions against Syria, which he termed a violation of international law, and that he will seek to reopen the Syrian Embassy. "I will be Syria's voice," SANA reports Black as stating.

During his three-day visit, Senator Black held in-depth discussions with the Speaker of the People's Assembly Mohammad Jihad al-Laham as well as other leading government and civilian leaders. On April 28, Iran's Press TV, its English-language service, prominently featured a report of Black's meeting with Syrian President Bashar al-Assad and his advisors in Damascus. In the television clips of the meeting, Black emphasized that what is happening in Syria bears no resemblance to the disinformation being spread by elements of the U.S. administration. In the same television coverage, President Assad is shown stating that terrorism knows no borders and that the fight against terror requires a joint international effort that is not limited to the military level.

The Larger Picture

Three weeks prior to Senator Black's trip to Syria, he delivered a speech to a conference sponsored by the Schiller Institute in New York City, titled "The Folly of U.S. Military Interventions in Iraq, Syria, and Libya Since 2011." In that presentation, Black delivered a thorough analysis of how, in the fifteen years since the 2001 9/11 attack, the United States and Great Britain have carried out a relentless campaign of regime-change carnage throughout the Arab world including, but not limited to the invasions of Iraq and Afghanistan, the murder of Libyan leader Muammar Qaddafi, a failed attempt to install a (British) Muslim Brotherhood regime in Egypt, and the continuing effort to overthrow the government of Syria and turn the country over to the hordes of ISIS (Daesh). Not only has none of this had anything to do with the perpetrators of 9/11, but the current effort to destroy Syria, Black stated, has placed the United States into a direct alliance with Turkey and Saudi Arabia, the two chief backers of terrorism in the region.

In his address, Black went on to emphasize the

Virginia State Senator Richard Black

EIRNS/Stuart Lewis

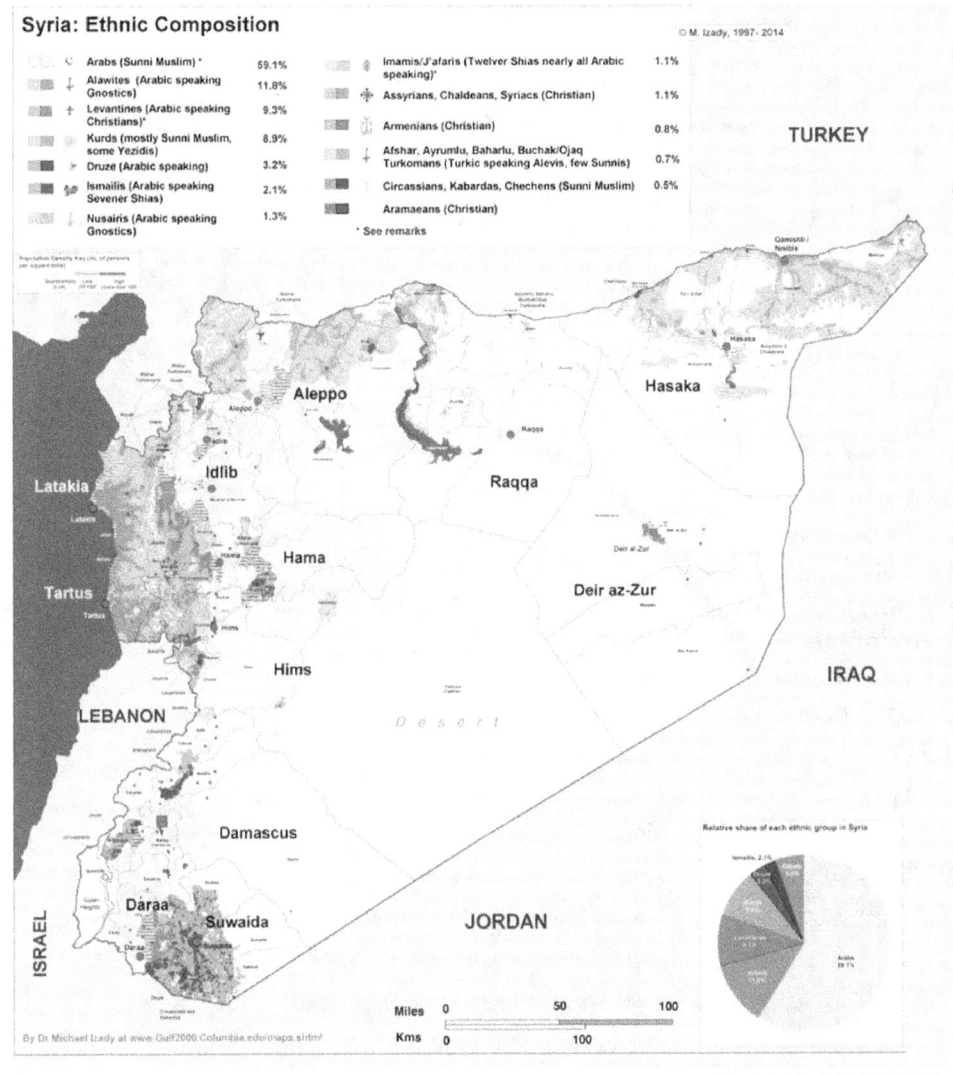

Syria: Ethnic Composition

© M. Izady, 1997-2014

Arabs (Sunni Muslim) *	59.1%	Imamis/J'afaris (Twelve Shias nearly all Arabic speaking)*	1.1%
Alawites (Arabic speaking Gnostics)	11.8%	Assyrians, Chaldeans, Syriacs (Christian)	1.1%
Levantines (Arabic speaking Christians)*	9.3%	Armenians (Christian)	0.8%
Kurds (mostly Sunni Muslim, some Yezidis)	8.9%	Afshar, Ayrumlu, Baharlu, Buchak/Ojaq Turkomans (Turkic speaking Alevis, few Sunnis)	0.7%
Druze (Arabic speaking)	3.2%	Circassians, Kabardas, Chechens (Sunni Muslim)	0.5%
Ismailis (Arabic speaking Sevener Shias)	2.1%	Aramaeans (Christian)	
Nusairis (Arabic speaking Gnostics)	1.3%	* See remarks	

By Dr. Michael Izady at www.Gulf2000.Columbia.edu/maps.shtml

Map by M. Izady/Gulf 2000 Project

The multi-religious and multi-ethnic character of Syria.

nage and suffering is horrific, but the larger implications are more horrible. In his interview with the Speaker al-Laham, as reported by SANA, Senator Black said that what is happening in Syria now affects the future of civilization for the entire world, that if the Syrian government were to lose the war, there would be devastating repercussions for civilization and humanity in general. Black stated that the steadfastness of a country like Syria in the face of all the American, European, and Arab Gulf powers is "a miracle from God." In reply, al-Laham stressed that Syria is combating terrorism and extremism on behalf of the whole world, and that victory over the armed terrorist organizations will be a victory for civil values for all people.

In another interview, Black said that the crisis in Syria did not start within the country, but rather in Western and Gulf capitals and their intelligence services, which made the decision to create chaos, and have done so, shedding much blood in the process. Black praised Russia's intervention into the war against terrorism, saying that it produced great changes in the dynamic in the region.

In a series of text messages from Black to the *Washington Post*, he further elaborated the reasons for his trip. According to the *Post*, Black stated, "I am hoping to move us away from our insane policy regarding Syria. Syria has greater women's rights and religious freedom than any nation in the Arab world," and, "We are allied with two of the most vile nations on Earth, Saudi Arabia and Turkey, which are intent on imposing a Wahhabi fundamentalist government on the Syrian people."

moral contradiction of this current alliance. Syria is a secular nation with a democratically elected government. Under the Assad government, all religious groups, including a sizable Christian minority, have free exercise of their faith, and the rights of women are the most advanced in the Arab world. Conversely, Saudi Arabia has never held an election, women have no rights, and beheadings and other forms of barbaric punishment are routinely carried out on both opponents of the monarchy and religious minorities.

What Is at Stake

More than 162,000 people have been killed in Syria since 2011, according to reports, and 11 million have fled Syria or have become refugees within it. This car-

Every Day Counts In Today's Showdown To Save Civilization

That's why you need EIR's **Daily Alert Service**, a strategic overview compiled with the input of Lyndon LaRouche, and delivered to your email 5 days a week.

For example: On Jan. 7, EIR's Daily Alert featured the British hand behind the pattern of global provocations toward war. Of special note is British Intelligence's role in instigating the Saudi Kingdom's attempt to set off a Sunni-Shia war. This religious war has been the intent of British strategy since the Blair-Bush attack on Iraq in 2003.

We also uniquely update you regularly on the progress toward the release of the suppressed 28 pages of the Congressional Inquiry on 9/11, which would expose the Saudi role.

Every edition highlights the reality of the impending financial crash/bail-in policies that would realize the British goal of mass depopulation.

This is intelligence you need to act on, if we are going to survive as a nation and a species. Can you really afford to be without it?

THURSDAY, JANUARY 7, 2016

Volume 2, Number 97

EIR Daily Alert Service

P.O. Box 17390, Washington, DC 20041-0390

- British Crown Pushing War and Genocide in 2016
- Financial Mudslide Goes On; Monetarist Tyranny Gloats over Bail-Ins
- Moody's Downgrades Portugal's Novo Banco
- Puerto Rico's Default: It's Every Vulture for Himself
- Wide Glass-Steagall Debate Set Off Again by Sanders Speech
- MI6 Mouthpiece Evans-Pritchard Touts Persian Gulf Chaos
- North Korea Tests a Miniaturized Hydrogen Bomb
- Uighur Terrorists Found in Indonesia
- Foreign Investors Are Flocking In to China

EDITORIAL

British Crown Pushing War and Genocide in 2016

II. Music and the Manhattan Project

LYNN YEN

The Mission of the Foundation for The Revival of Classical Culture

May 2—Dennis Speed of the LaRouche Manhattan Project interviewed Lynn J. Yen, Director of the Foundation for the Revival of Classical Culture, on April 29.

Dennis Speed: Let's talk about what the Foundation for the Revival of Classical Culture has been doing for the last year in New York City. There has been a lot of work at schools and with young people. Can you describe it?

Lynn Yen: Yes. This year we started an outreach program of bringing concert artists into the public schools, of bringing classical music to a lot more young people. What we have done thus far is to invite a number of concert artists, pianists, cellists, violinists, vocalists, and classical musicians of all kinds to come and visit these schools, where we organize for whole classrooms and, actually, for the whole school to be assembled, where the musicians present musical performances, and talk to these young people about what is music, what is classical music, what is classical culture, and what is this music that they have just played for them, followed by questions and answers. We have so far visited, or been involved in, about 43 public schools.

We have had some extraordinary feedback from

EIRNS/Stuart Lewis

Lynn Yen addressing a Schiller Institute Conference in New York, January 2013.

kids and teachers, but very especially teachers. For example, there was a teacher in a school in Queens who, after one of our sopranos sang at the school, sent us a wonderful email, saying how appreciative she was that we included her school in the program, and how appreciative they were to have the kids so benefitted from the wonderful presentation—and it wasn't just a performance, but an actual presentation.

We had one baritone, for example, who went to a public school, a middle school, and when we went into the school the parent coordinator said, "You're the classical music people! I'm so excited! But I have to tell you, these kids only like hip-hop, and you might have difficulties." But when the baritone started singing from Handel's *Messiah*, I believe it was the second solo, about the coming of the Prophet, there was such a look of concentration on all of the faces of these fourth and fifth graders; they were completely captivated by the music, and they were captivated for the whole presentation—the whole piece, definitely, but the whole presentation—because he introduced other music to them. They asked lots of questions. At the end, one of the kids said, "Can you just please sing some more?"

We have had teachers who have written to us, as

one from a middle school, where the teacher said, after we did the visit, that one student in particular, who has been hard to engage in the past, told her that he really enjoyed it, and asked when the musician would come back again. And she said, "For me, watching the students, who at first are taken aback by an operatic voice—they giggle a little in the beginning, then quickly become interested and excited—was particularly gratifying. I think having opportunities to encounter something like this, to engage with and enjoy it is so incredibly important and powerful for our kids. "

I think we need to continue to do this, and to give this to a lot more young people in a lot of schools. Because just with these 43 schools we have been in throughout Manhattan, Brooklyn, Queens, and the Bronx, we have been in front of over 17,000 young people, and we want to translate that now into something more substantial.

On Easter Sunday, March 27, 2016, the LaRouche Manhattan Project and the Foundation for the Revival of Classical Culture collaborated in the performance of parts II and III of Handel's Messiah *at the Church of the Visitation of the Blessed Virgin Mary in Brooklyn.*

Speed: What you just said, that you have been in front of 17,000 young people in 43 schools, how many people does that mean are in these different sessions? It sounds like they must be pretty large.

Yen: Yes. Usually a school will be between 300 and 800 people. We would break the sessions down to half the school, usually the upper and lower grades. In some rare instances we have had the whole school together. But we always make sure it is of a size that will allow the kids to really be part of the program, and not just part of some very large, large performance.

Speed: How are these programs composed?

Yen: It is usually about 45 minutes to an hour, essentially one school period. The teachers will coordinate so that certain grades of certain schools will come into the auditorium, or in one case, where we had a Ukrainian pianist and cellist, it was in the basement, so the kids all sat around the pianist and cellist. The musicians prepare two or three or four pieces; in the case of that basement, it was two pieces, one by Beethoven, one by Franck.

Typically, with the instrumental pieces, which are longer, the musicians will perform one or two movements from it. They would say something about the music first, invite questions first, and then answer questions later. In the case of some of the singers, because they are singing in a language other than English—German, Italian, and French—they explain the piece beforehand, sometimes asking the students to pronounce a certain word in that language and ask them to listen for it, and then afterwards answer questions. It is a very interactive type of program.

Handel's *Messiah*

Speed: From the inception of the foundation you have been talking about performing the Handel *Messiah*. There have been several performances of the *Messiah*. Why did you emphasize this from the beginning of the foundation, and what has happened with the use of the *Messiah* over the years?

Yen: First of all, we emphasized the performance of Handel's *Messiah* because it is written in English. It is in many ways one of the most accessible pieces of classical music for English speakers today. It has many aspects that make it wonderful. Handel wrote it in 24 days, and he wrote it with an intention to help others. He wrote it originally [for a benefit performance] to get people out of debtors' prison, and for the poor and the sick.

Messiah gives the listeners hope, gives them the promise of a better and brighter future. More importantly, you have to look at what the United States and what our culture today is doing and not doing. There is so much violence in America. There is so much violence, for example, in the schools, in the youth population. There is so much darkness. What is so important about Handel's *Messiah*? To put it in context, as Martin Luther King once said, "As great as are the stars in Heaven, as great as the music of Handel's *Messiah*, how much greater is the mind of man that contemplates these things?"

That is the really important thing, because I think that Handel's *Messiah* celebrates the really important aspect, the divine creativity that lies in every human being; if people can come to realize that, that is essential for their own humanity. What does the *Messiah* talk about? It talks about love, it talks about forgiveness, it talks about peace, unity, all the things we need in America, in the world today—the elevation of all of ourselves to the idea of love. Again, Dr. King said that the principle of nonviolence is the principle of love.

To Bring People Together in Love

We originally started four years ago with the idea of performing Handel's *Messiah*. It has been a long road, and we still have a long way to go. But last December we performed Handel's *Messiah* twice, once in Brooklyn and once in Manhattan, parts one and two. This was in collaboration with the Schiller Institute Community Chorus, which was started December 20, 2014, exactly a year before our concert this past December,

www.tongji.edu.cn

Even though frenetic hip-hop and crazed rock music have spread globally, including to China, Yen noted that Classical presentations by her Foundation demonstrated an ability of young students to concentrate that was not expected by their teachers. Above, a contemplative young audience in China listening to Classical music.

precisely because on December 20, 2014, two policemen were killed in Brooklyn as we were performing Handel's *Messiah* for the first time, a much smaller concert. At the dinner after that performance in 2014, the conductor and I, and the soloists and a few others said, well, something has to be done to bring people together as a community, to bring people together in love.

It came about a year later. There were two concerts, performed on December 19 and 20, and we had a full house for both concerts. It was overfilled at the Manhattan location. A lot of young people and families came to those concerts, and I think people want to be part of something that uplifts them, that shows them that there is a different path, a more beautiful path to life.

On Easter this year, March 27, we presented parts two and three of the *Messiah*. We performed at the Church of the Visitation of the Blessed Virgin Mary, because when storm Sandy hit New York especially hard [in October 2012], that was where much of the concentration of the effort to help the city took place. We wanted to do something for the community again to bring people together around something that is a higher idea, and of course, there is a beautiful idea of resurrection in Easter.

The Importance of Proper Tuning

The three concerts in 2015-2016 were all, very importantly, performed at the proper or Verdi tuning of C=256 herz (cycles per second), or you could call it A=432. It is a very important point, because vocally, musically, when you have a great classical composition performed at the proper tuning, it not only allows the real power and majesty and beauty of the music to come to the fore, it allows the audience to much more easily hear the real idea of the music and to understand what it is really saying. We are hoping to do more of this.

Speed: You did a series of concerts at Carnegie Hall, and you have done these concerts at the proper tuning. Can you say something about that, and also about the concert of 2015 which was dedicated against violence?

Yen: Starting in 2013, when I realized the importance of the proper tuning in musical and artistic performance of, especially, classical compositions, we had our first Carnegie Hall concert, on May 28, 2013, at Zankel Hall, Carnegie Hall. We titled it *Properly Tuned Masterpieces* and pianist Tian Jiang performed. It was very interesting, because Leszek,[1] the Grammy Award winning sound engineer at Carnegie Hall, said to me that what he heard of Tian's performance of the Chopin *Nocturnes* was so bel canto, so vocal, so "singing" in its music, that he's never heard anything like it before. He said, "I'm Polish, and Chopin's favorite composer is Bellini, so Chopin is always composing his music with the idea of vocalization of his instrumental, his piano pieces, and to hear it like this was really wonderful."

So I came to realize the importance of the proper tuning, or what everybody knows as the "Verdi tuning."

---

1. Leszek M. Wojcik, Recording Studio Manager of Carnegie Hall, has been at Carnegie for over 30 years. He has recorded most of the world's great pianists—Brendel, Horowitz, and Schiff, among others. He knows more about recording in Carnegie Hall than almost anyone else alive. —Dennis Speed

We then did subsequent concerts, including the very important one on June 21, 2015, Fathers' Day, and it was titled "Music Against Violence, and Music of the Future," because, again, it is really important for us to remind people, for us to do something that is not simply some concert, but something that has real meaning. What is the purpose of music? What is the purpose of culture? The purpose is to make people better people. If you can't do that, you are not doing the right thing. You are not doing things that are really, truly, meaningful.

Love Against Hate

This concert was our attempt to again bring young people together, and in this case we had in the audience over 1,700 young people and their parents and teachers, and this was from more than 80 schools, who came to this concert on Fathers' Day—especially on Fathers' Day, because so many of our young men and fathers have been killed meaninglessly. Since 9/11 there have not been many people killed by terrorism, but there have been 500 or more killed by violence in New York City. What should one do about that?

Representatives of the New York Police Department participated in this concert, and we had among the speakers during the intermission, Terry Strada, who is the Chairwoman of the 9/11 Families United for Justice Against Terrorism, and Dr. Bernard Lafayette, who is the successor to Dr. King as head of the Southern Christian Leadership Conference. He is the chairman of the board. He is also the head of the National Center for Creative Nonviolence.

Dr. Lafayette and Mrs. Strada both talked about the importance of love against hate, of how important music is. Dr. Lafayette said, for example, that it was crucial for the Civil Rights Movement. In his brief remarks he made a really clear point about the role of music and that it enabled the Civil Rights Movement to function and be successful. He emphasized how much today billions of people around the world need this music of freedom, which can never be sung by violence.

Mrs. Strada said it is necessary that we see beyond the hatred and practice a more beautiful culture. This is something that is vital today; it is especially vital that we continue to work toward that spirit of man, and to work to inspire that spirit of man in ourselves and among all people, but especially among young people.

JOHN SIGERSON

The Meaning of Schumann's *Dichterliebe* Song Cycle

April 30—Dennis Speed interviewed Schiller Institute Music Director John Sigerson today.

Dennis Speed: What is the role of the Schumann song cycle, *Dichterliebe*, in musical history? Why did you pick this piece to perform at the Schiller Institute's Manhattan Conference of April 7?

John Sigerson: The *Dichterliebe* cycle is but one of the veritable cornucorpia of fruits of Robert Schumann's *Liederjahr*, his "song year," 1840. In the years leading up to this, Schumann had been composing primarily piano music; many of these compositions were collections of pieces that you could also call cycles without words. And indeed, in one of these he explicitly references the opening theme of one of the very first true song cycles, namely Beethoven's *An die ferne Geliebte* (To the Distant Beloved), composed 24 years earlier. In the intervening time, Beethoven's admirer Franz Schubert composed his two famous cycles, *Die schöne Müllerin* (The Beautiful Miller's Daughter) and *Winterreise* (Winter's Journey).

But what distinguishes Schumann's *Dichterliebe* is the incredible unity of effect he achieves with only 16 songs, some of them less than a minute long. From the very first note of the first song—a C-sharp by the way—there's an unbroken chain of poetic tension that doesn't let up until the dying-out of the final note, which happens to be a D-flat—which is the same note on the keyboard, but with transformed significance, which pulls the entire cycle together.

When I was asked to sing for the conference, my thoughts went to a song cycle, and not just one or two songs, because I wanted to conclude the event not with relaxing entertainment, but with a real moral challenge, in keeping with the overall purpose of conference, namely to encourage participants to take political *and* moral responsibility for ensuring that mankind will not only survive as a species, but will have a future worth living. And in the *Dichterliebe*, the poet-singer must confront dark corners of his soul, before finally, in the last song, he is able to laugh at himself and, as he

EIRNS/Stuart Lewis

John Sigerson singing the Dichterliebe *song cycle by Robert Schumann at the April 7 Schiller Institute Conference in New York, "Building a World Land-Bridge: Realizing Mankind's True Humanity." He is accompanied by Yegor Shevstov.*

says explicitly, bury his "old songs"!

The Classical Outlook

Speed: The *Dichterliebe* is popularly referred to as exemplary of the Romantic School of poetic and musical composition. Why do you insist that the reality is quite the opposite?

Sigerson: Well, the first thing you have to understand, is that contrary to the history textbooks, music is not divided up into "periods" characterized by different "styles." As Friedrich Schiller argued in his celebrated lecture on universal history, history is not merely a succession of periods or strings of events, but rather it is the history of millennia of struggle between, on the one side, man's creative

The poet Heinrich Heine composed the lyrics to Dichterliebe.

impulse, which distinguishes him absolutely from the beasts, and on the other side, those oligarchical institutions and individuals which insist that, on the contrary, man *is* essentially a beast, and that creativity must be checked whenever it threatens those institutions.

Classical music is therefore not a style, but rather what Lyndon LaRouche has described as a "mind-set," a *Weltanschauung* which gives absolute priority to human creativity as a vehicle for ennobling mankind, making him happier and more productive in discovering and mastering universal principles—principles of a developing, living universe.

The poet Heinrich Heine, who composed the lyrics to *Dichterliebe*, developed himself into a scholar of this mind-set, and in his major work, *The History of Religion and Philosophy in Germany*, he points out that the so-called "Romantic School" was in fact spawned by the philosopher Immanuel Kant, who argued that true creativity is essentially unknowable, and that humans are necessarily slaves to their own emotions, curbed only by social rules or maxims. In other words, man is essentially a trainable animal.

Schumann knew and loved not only Heine's poetry, but also his political and philosophical writings, and any fair reading of both Heine's poems and Schumann's setting of them, will confirm that what is being discussed here, is nothing less than the underlying conflict I've just outlined.

Metaphor and Irony

Speed: Lyndon LaRouche has emphasized the polemical nature of this music, and that if the performance is properly done, and the audience is attentive, they will be moved to laughter or to deep irritation, but not left indifferent. Why?

Sigerson: Well, if it were merely polemical and nothing else, it wouldn't be art. A more precise way to look at it, is from the standpoint of metaphor, that is, the ironical juxtaposition of elements which don't seem to fit together "in the small," but which create a motion—or perhaps better, an emotion—moving toward the discovery of a higher moral truth. And as Schiller insists, all this must clothed in beauty, because a certain suspension of the ugliness of the everyday world is necessary to elevate men's souls.

This sort of metaphor is the principle underlying the counterpoint of J.S. Bach—which many of his contemporaries found so objectionable, and which is totally rejected by today's so-called popular music. But not only that: Even the best music of Bach, Beethoven, Schubert, Schumann, and Brahms completely loses its "clout" if it is performed from any standpoint other than this. That is why so much purportedly Classical music performed today is so mind-numbingly boring.

In the Twentieth Century, one individual who knew this well, and got into lots of trouble for it, was the conductor and composer Wilhelm Furtwängler. For him, there was no separation between the developing universe, and the thinking, creative human mind. His music had such power, that even Adolf Hitler was terrified of him!

The Schumanns and their extended network of associates were all dedicated to music as the communication of profound ideas and principles.

music as essentially the communication of profound ideas and principles. They were resolutely opposed to music as mere novel effects, which the oligarchical circles of the day were promoting with their first "rock stars," such as violin acrobat Niccolo Paganini and the piano-destroyer Franz Liszt.

As for other works, of course there are many! Another favorite of mine is Schumann's very first song cycle, his Opus 24, also a series of settings of what Heine liked to term his "little poison poems." One other poet whose creations Brahms often set to music was Eduard Mörike, who is less well known, but who is one of Helga Zepp-LaRouche's favorites. One other thing that Brahms particularly liked to do, was to take a piece of inferior Romantic poetry, and to give it a totally Classical treatment. His *Die schöne Magelone* cycle is a good example of that.

And I might add, Furtwängler sometimes did the same thing, most famously with his 1938 recording of Tchaikovsky's Symphony No. 6, called the "Pathétique." The young Lyndon LaRouche, upon hearing this recording while stationed in India at the close of World War II, was stunned at how Furtwängler had managed to completely rid the work of its "soap opera" tendencies, and, through ironic juxtapositions, elevate it to the level of the Classical in Schiller's sense.

Furtwängler as Composer

Speed: Furtwängler and his role in the Twentieth Century have defined your own approach to orchestral and choral conducting, and you have in the last two years done several performances, including the Mozart *Requiem* and Handel's *Messiah*, in an attempt to convey "the Furtwängler principle" to larger audiences. But Furtwängler, as a pianist, also worked with singers of German *Lieder*, such as Dietrich Fischer-Dieskau and Elisabeth Schwarzkopf. Is his approach to working with an individual great singer the same, or different, than his approach to the orchestra? And what does that identity or difference in approach tell us about his unique approach to music?

Sigerson: Furtwängler considered himself to be a composer first and foremost. He composed *Lieder*, an oratorio, a symphonic concerto, violin sonatas, and

The *Davidsbund*

Speed: Schumann and Heine were friends, as were Felix Mendelssohn, his sister Fanny, and several others; they made up the artistic grouping Schumann called the *Davidsbund* [a reference to King David's league that fought the Philistines —ed.]. What does the *Dichterliebe* as a project express about their outlook? Were there other works of this type, whether by Schumann and Heine, or by others?

Sigerson: Yes, this was an extended circle of friends and associates which, by the way, included the American System economist Friedrich List, who for some years was Schumann's neighbor in Leipzig. Then young Johannes Brahms showed up one day on Schumann's doorstep, and became part of the family, too. Along with Schumann's wife Clara, they were all dedicated to

Any success I may have had so far in conveying Furtwängler's mind-set, said Sigerson, has been more due to the overall social and political context of our performances.

into all his performance work, whether it was *Lieder*, opera, or symphonic works. For him, greatness in performance lay not in technical perfection, but rather in greatness of heart and mind and a oneness of moral purpose—which is why, for example, he preferred his "scrappy" Berlin Philharmonic to other more technically refined orchestras.

I must confess that any success I may have had so far in conveying Furtwängler's mind-set has been more due to the overall social and political context of the performances you mentioned, and also to our well-prepared chorus, than to the orchestras, since we have never had the

three symphonies. He viewed his conducting as a necessary and important sideline, and it always pained him that the public put his conducting before his composing. His creative compositional impulse flowed equally

luxury of the extended rehearsal time required to bring all the instrumentalists into agreement with my intention. But I look forward to the happy day when that will be possible.

LaRouche Policy Committee Statement

KESHA ROGERS

A Unified Mission for the Common Aims of Mankind

May 3—On April 24, China celebrated its first official National Space Day. Russia celebrated Yuri's Night, honoring Yuri Gagarin, the first man to fly into space, on April 12. But despite America's former leadership in space exploration, the United States has no national day of recognition for our entry into the Space Age, marked by Alan Shepard's historic space flight. Shepard was the second human being and the first American to fly in space, on May 5, 1961, soon followed by John Glenn—flights that led to the realization of President John F. Kennedy's vision to land a man on the Moon and return him safely to Earth.

No, in the United States we don't have a national space day, we just have Americans who are spaced out. The fact that there is not an adequate fight coming from the scientific community and the American people to demand the immediate removal of Obama—for his continued policies that destroy our space program and the future of our nation—shows that the people have given up on the vision for a true future for our nation and the generations to come. That commitment must be restored now!

China and Russia are not celebrating their respective national space days just because they want to celebrate the achievements of a single person or event; no, these days reflect the achievements of a nation and its commitment to the future, the commitment to those not yet born, to advances in science, and the discoveries that still await us.

The deputy commander of China's Manned Space Program, Lt. Gen. Zhang Yulin, announced on China's National Space Day that China plans to land astronauts on the Moon by 2036. Zhang remarked, "China must

LaRouche PAC TV

Here, standing in front of the statue of Confucius in Houston's Rose Garden on April 24, LaRouche Policy Committee member Kesha Rogers congratulates China for establishing a national day to celebrate its entry into the Space Age.

raise its abilities and use the next 15 to 20 years to realize manned lunar exploration goals, and take a firm step for the Chinese people in breaking ground in the utilization of space."

Seize the Opportunity for Mankind

China's President Xi Jinping encouraged scientists and engineers on National Space Day to "seize the strategic opportunity and keep innovating to make a greater contribution to the country's overall growth and the welfare of mankind." That day, China made a point, a very important point, of inviting the United states to collaborate in the development of space, as it had also done in the offer to cooperate in the development of the Silk Road and what Xi has called a policy of "win-win."

Instead of accepting this offer of cooperation, Obama—on behalf of the British/Saudi empire, whose murderous policies he continues to defend—is escalating the drive towards nuclear war and total chaos. Not only is the Obama Administration continuing to escalate with military exercises in the South China Sea, bringing future increased tensions between the United States and China, but it is also instigating an insane NATO policy of heightening tensions with Russia as our forces move nearer to its borders, provoking the threat of war.

Stop the FBI, Restore JFK's Vision

For the decades since the assassination of President Kennedy, but going back even further to the death of President Franklin Roosevelt, the people of the United States have been held in a choke hold by the thuggish tactics of the FBI to frighten people into submission, going after anyone who tries to put up a fight for creativity and discovery. The policy of the FBI and the British has been to destroy any remaining commitment in the United States to real scientific progress and to force those in the scientific community to accept the idea that they are impotent and without any means to fight for a true mission for our nation in the exploration and development of space.

The advances and creative discoveries of mankind in space exploration are our strongest and most vital achievements in securing the potential for peace among nations, an idea which President Kennedy truly understood and expressed in his inaugural address when he said,

So let us begin anew—remembering on both sides that civility is not a sign of weakness, and sincerity is always subject to proof. Let us never negotiate out of fear. But let us never fear to negotiate. Let both sides explore what problems unite us instead of belaboring those problems which divide us....

Let both sides seek to invoke the wonders of science instead of its terrors. Together let us explore the stars, conquer the deserts, eradicate disease, tap the ocean depths, and encourage the arts and commerce.

Let both sides unite to heed in all corners of the earth the command of Isaiah—to 'undo the heavy burdens . . . [and] let the oppressed go free.'

And if a beach-head of cooperation may push back the jungle of suspicion, let both sides join in creating a new endeavor, not a new balance of power, but a new world of law, where the strong are just and the weak secure and the peace preserved....

Now the trumpet summons us again—not as a call to bear arms, though arms we need—not as a call to battle, though embattled we are—but a call to bear the burden of a long twilight struggle, year in and year out, 'rejoicing in hope, patient in tribulation'—a struggle against the common enemies of man: tyranny, poverty, disease and war itself.

Today, the only chance we have to restore peace among all nations is to remove Obama now and shut down the Empire and its bankrupt trans-Atlantic and Wall Street system that is destroying the possibility of progress. We must restore the principles of true scientific progress, which our American system of economy was founded on, under Alexander Hamilton. Those are the principles which China has adopted as it leads in the exploration of space, starting with its remarkable mission to explore and develop the far side of the Moon, leading to potential breakthroughs in such areas as the mining of helium 3 and radio imaging of the universe.

We ask again today, as President Kennedy first asked, "Can we forge against these enemies [tyranny, poverty, disease, and war] a grand and global alliance, North and South, East and West, that can assure a more fruitful life for all mankind? Will you join in that historic effort?"

The answer to that question, my friends, depends on you. A unified mission for advancing the common aims of mankind and the development of the creative powers of all children, must be brought into being now. That is the intention and purpose for which mankind pursues the exploration of space.

www.ingramcontent.com/pod-product-compliance
Lightning Source LLC
Chambersburg PA
CBHW081203280526
45787CB00008B/3389